Frugal Simplicity

101 Ways To Use Frugal Simplicity For Organizing And Decluttering Your Life And Embracing The Simplicity Lifestyle For Greater Personal Finances And Freedom!

I0464957

Lilly Sparks

STOP!!! Before you read any further....Would you like to know the secrets of Anti-Aging?

If your answer is yes, then you are not alone. Thousands of people are looking for the secret to reducing wrinkles, looking younger, and maintaining a youthful appearance.

If you have been searching for these answers without much luck, you are in the right place!

Not only will you gain incredible insight in this book, but because I want to make sure to give you as much value as possible, right now for a limited time you can get full **100% FREE access to a VIP bonus EBook** entitled **Anti-Aging Made Easy!**

Just Go Here For Free Instant Access:

www.LuxyLifeNaturals.com

Legal Notice

Disclaimer Notice

Table Of Contents

Introduction

I want to thank you and congratulate you for purchasing the book, *Frugal Simplicity: 101 Ways To Use Frugal Simplicity For Organizing And Decluttering Your Life And Embracing The Simplicity Lifestyle For Greater Personal Finances And Freedom.*

Do you know what many successful people have in common? Apart from leading stress-free and happy lives and achieving their goals in life, they have a secret; they value the importance of frugality.

The fact is, dealing with problems such as not having time for family and friends, not having any money during emergencies, and even not having sufficient sleep may often be as a result of poor work ethics, poor decision-making, poor habits and poor strategizing. If you think there is no escape out of your messy life, you are wrong. There is a solution, and you can get started by familiarizing yourself with frugal simplicity.

Thanks again for purchasing this book, I hope you enjoy it!

Chapter 1: How To Be Frugal And Save Money

As defined on numerous sites, frugality is about knowing how to live accordingly by not allowing food, money, supplies, and mostly anything to go to waste. Some would argue that it is about fleeing from lavishness and being a cheapskate. Well, it is not. Rather, it is about wisely making the most out of what you have. Should things unfold according to your plans, heaps of joys in the form of self-fulfillment along with financial security are bound to come your way.

1 – Go for the Original

Buy original items, instead of there more affordable counterparts. On occasion, there are necessary purchases including a car tire, faucet, cabinets, and beds. A way to save? Choose the genuine kinds. Usually, they are more expensive but they are cost-effective (i.e. built with quality, minimal maintenance needed and sturdy).

2 – NO to Waste

Use resources wisely. Have you been advised to turn off the lights during the day? How about preparing a glass of water to use when brushing your teeth? Or, replacing your lights to energy-efficient bulbs? The reminders are probably redundant but you have to pay attention anyway. They can be a huge help in reducing the total costs of your monthly utility (electricity, energy, and water) bills.

3 – All You Need Is One (Card)

Consolidate credit and debit cards. Owning multiple accounts costs big so make sure your salary can afford to pay off the regular fees that come with them. If not, determine measures to have just one.

4 – It's a Sale, It's a Sale!

Take advantage of stores' sales. During one, you can avail of huge discounts. So, if you are thinking of buying that sofa for $400, check whether a sale is in order. Until then, put off your purchase. If you are lucky, that item will be yours for $200.

5 – A Long, Windy Road

Aim for long-term goals instead of living for the moment (paycheck to paycheck). Buy what you truly like (be it costly) in favor of what you can currently afford. Joy comes with achieving a goal, regardless of how small it is but the bigger the goal, the bigger the reward is.

6 – No to Gimmicky Insurance Deals

Avoid signing up for insurance gimmicks. Insurance agents may come to you with great deals such as accidental death double indemnity and short-term health insurance. Since they are usually expensive, say no to the temptation. While they could be promising, chances are, you would not need them and you would not benefit from them.

#7 – On The Record

Keep track of all your typical expenses for food, transportation, and extras. Assess how much you usually spend each day. This way, you can start setting a limit for your daily expenses the following week.

8 - Just You

Focus on yourself, rather than focusing on something that another person possesses. For example, your neighbor bought a new phone. Instead of envying him, pay attention to your own wants and your own needs.

9 – The Whole and Not Just the Parts

Buy goods in bulk - especially ones you consume regularly such as rice, coffee, and powdered milk. For one, bulk-buying grants discounts. For another, you'll save on transportation cost.

10 – Save, Save, Save

Stop purchasing items you want but will not use. Be meticulous and avoid letting a cent go to waste.

Chapter 2: Steps To Declutter Your Life In General

Do you tend to be all over the place almost all the time? Call it fun. Call it spontaneity. Call it an adventure. But, you have to admit, you know it means one thing: you have a cluttered life.

While there may be exciting perks and surprises to it, there are also setbacks to a cluttered life. Suffice it to say, you'll have less time on your hands. You won't have time to: visit family and friends, walk your dog, enjoy a savory meal, look after yourself, and many more. Rather than keep living in an unorderly fashion, begin cleaning your mess as soon as possible.

11 - Work, Work, Work

Like it or not, you have to go to work. Since working is an effective way to earn regular income for you to afford all the necessities (and even luxuries), it is a ticket to a clutter-free life.

12 - You Are My Friend

Choose your friends. Having people around can create clutter in your life but you can have a say on the kind of clutter you will be dealing with. Turn away from those who refuse you to draw positive vibes because if you keep hanging out with negative buddies, your perspective in life will also become negative.

13 - Like Water

Move on. Accept the fact that things change over time. It could be a person, a hobby, a relationship, a game, or an old special place you insist on visiting regularly. Remember, if something is not of substantial, leave it behind.

14 – One at a Time

Learn to concentrate on a single task. Avoid carrying a load and avoid juggling things. For example, ten tasks are on your list. If you attend to all of them simultaneously, chances are, a confusing life is ahead of you.

15 – Debt No More

Start figuring out a way to pay back the people you owe money to. The thing with having a debt is that it is unlikely to give you peace of mind. Try as you may but unless you no longer have some unfinished business, you cannot be at ease.

16 – Let It Be Okay

Be okay with the fact that you do not (and maybe cannot) have all the things you want. Rather than go through life with a bitter attitude, see matters with a fresh light.

17 - Conformity Is an Enemy

Appreciate the power in saying NO. If you disagree with a concept, turn back from it. Perhaps, you received an invite to a concert or you were encouraged to buy a new appliance, and you intend to pass, you should decline. If you do not want to, for whatever reason, that is your prerogative.

18 – Should You Invest?

Invest only in items you know you can afford to pay. Investments of all sizes are often good. However, you have to be realistic and avoid generating accounts you are likely to abandon in the near future.

19 – Breakaway

Take a break regularly. Once in a while, do the things you enjoy. Go somewhere far; spend a day with your friends, or anything that makes you feel good. Doing so allows you to restore order and have a balanced outlook of life.

20 – Health Is Wealth

Value your health. Eat right, exercise, and get sufficient amount of sleep. Other than the fact that you can think about your life clearly when you are in good condition, you can evade a stack of costly medical bills by staying well.

Chapter 3: Tips To Organize Your Life

Did you know that many people - from busy corporate professionals to ordinary individuals on the street - have made it big in their pursuits by making sure they have organized lives? What these people have in common is that although they have a load of things to do every day, they still seem to keep things in order.

With an unorganized life like theirs, you'll tend to be more familiar with who and how you are. Instead of getting surprised by the stacks of uncertainties and even financial problems that can come your way, you know exactly how to have a handle on things.

21 - A Schedule!

Jot down all the tasks you have to do. Whether it is for today, tomorrow, or the following day, having a list of your duties helps you remember.

22 – First Things First

Determine your priorities. Ask yourself what the most important things in your life are. Once you have matters sorted out, accommodate them first. If you have extra time to spare, you get back to little affairs.

23 – NO to Procrastination

Avoid putting off things. If you have to buy new sheets, visit a family member, play tennis with a colleague, or confront a friend, do it as soon as possible. Not only does the practice set matters in order, it also saves you from the trouble that can come with delays.

24 – Updating Yourself

Arrange your affairs regularly. Other than just having a schedule, anticipate the fact that unexpected events can arise. By sorting things out from time to time, you are creating a Plan B, given Plan A does not work out.

25 – Man Up!

Attend to responsibilities. As challenging and time-consuming they can be, you cannot ditch them if you want a mess-free life.

26 – Go for the Real Gold

Reach for workable pursuits. Before chasing after a goal, assess your capabilities. Be your own hero and prevent the heartache of not getting the result you were aiming for.

27 – Surely and Certainly

Be decisive. Ask yourself questions along the lines of *"Will I show up to the party?"*, *"Am I going to purchase that new coffee table?"*, and *"Should I dine at a fancy restaurant tonight?"* Make up your mind and stick to it.

28 – Flexibility Wins

Be willing to change. As much as you do not want them to, matters can turn the other direction. For you to have an organized life, try not to rebel against things that are going with the flow.

29 – This, too, Shall Pass

Stop worrying about things you have no control over. For instance, your favorite vase was accidently knocked over by your sister. You may be sad for a while but remind yourself to get over it and just purchase a new vase as the solution.

30 – Reality vs. the Internet

Limit the time you spend on social networking sites. 1 hour can be enough. As fun and exciting as they can be, sometimes they distract you of the more urgent things to mind.

Chapter 4: The Art Of Simplicity

As other people's definition go, simplicity is the practice of valuing the important things in life and preferring to eliminate anything else. So long as they have enough food, clothes, and a home, among many things, they are satisfied. They can and would be more interested to get by with nothing but the basics. By appreciating the simple pleasures in life rather than focusing on wanting to have more, you tend to become more effective and more productive.

31 - Fruits and Veggies

Set a day in a week where you eat nothing but fruits and vegetables (and drink nothing but water, too). As studies show, doing so is good for your physical and mental health. Additionally, since you are targeting to adopt a simple and frugal lifestyle, a basic healthy diet goes according to plan.

32 - Used, But Excellent, Nonetheless

Visit a store that sells used items that are still in excellent quality. For instance, if you need to buy a simple chair, be on the lookout for one at a used store. So long as it is from a reliable supplier, you are on the right track.

33 – What's in Front of You

Appreciate what you have. Instead of searching for items that could add more value to your life, be grateful for possessions that are already with you.

34 – Too Much Information

Quit overthinking since it can prevent you from viewing matters from an unbiased perspective. To live according to your own preferences, you need to incorporate a peaceful attitude.

35 – A Smile Can Go a Long Way

Wear a happy face. To learn to adopt and adapt to simple life, you should appreciate simple pleasures like smiling. Try to put to rest frowning sessions. Apart from that, it makes another happy.

36 – A Garden of Your Own

Take time off to garden. Learn about cultivating flowers, plants and vegetables. Remember, gardening is one of the most useful, simplest, and healthiest exercises. Aside from being a worthwhile activity, it is free (granted a housemate already owns a garden) allows you to breathe in fresh air.

37 – You Made It

Make handicrafts. From the used items and accessories at home, create place mats, table decorations, and other ornaments. Rather than shop for new items, rely on your creative skills.

38 – Treat the Little Creatures

Take your pet out for a walk. For one, your pet will adore you more for it; for another, it reduces stress.

39 – On Your Own

Be by yourself regularly. For your mind, it is healthy. Being alone enables you to evaluate your life from an unbiased perspective.

40 – Talk

Talk about your problems, instead of carrying ill feelings against another. Sorting out issues is a simple yet effective solution to being drowned by your emotions.

Chapter 5: How To Be Happy With Less Stuff

Many people seem to be at their happiest despite not having a fortune. Ironic, isn't it? As Robert Browning, in his poem, *The Faultless Painter* puts it, what can truly make you happy and content with life can be found within you, and not with your possessions. Learn the value of making do with just what you need in various aspects of your life.

41 - Food No More

Once you are full, avoid eating more. Remember, the objective is to simply have enough. Let your body be happy with less, too.

42 - Recycle

Re-use items, rather than toss them in a garbage bin. If you have no for them per se, think about whether you could still take advantage of the parts.

43 - It's about Creativity

Just because your belongings are old does not mean they cannot bring you joy. Let loose your creative side and make items interesting.

44 - NO to Getting Lucky

Avoid gambling. Turn your back on playing the lottery or the sweepstakes. There is nothing wrong with wanting to try your luck. However, to live a frugal life, you have to set the habit aside. For one, tickets are expensive, which may only dawn on you eventually; for another, all they are likely to do is keep your hopes.

45 - A Single Line Is Enough

Give away all your other phones. As the trend goes nowadays, owning multiple devices is almost a norm. Rather than go with the flow, just have one.

46 – Money at a Distance

Keep your money at the bank. This habit trains you not to make impulsive purchases. Likely, in a year's time, it will feel natural. Instead of having it in front of you (or somewhere you can easily have access), let it be at a safe distant.

47 – Hobbies!

Engage in your hobbies. Jog, play badminton, or swim. To encourage you to focus on the more important things, be occupied with your favorite activities.

48 – Temporarily Yours

Borrow items you know you will just use once. Especially if the said items will just be thrown away later, look for somebody else who can let you have it for a while.

49 – Less Is More

Talk less. It cuts down stress. Avoid investing your time talking too much, and instead, listen.

50 – See It for Real

Turn off the TV. Staying at home all day may not be best for you. Watch your favorite shows with a limit: 2-3 episodes will do. After, go out and enjoy the perks of real life.

Chapter 6: A Minimalist Lifestyle

In most cases, a person who lives simply and does not follow hectic routines could be recognized as a minimalist. Rather than go with the flow, she insists on standing on her own ground by living off plain and mundane choices in favor of the extravagant lifestyle. Consequently, she finds freedom in having complications eliminated.

51 - The Movie Theatre Is at Home

Watch a movie at home, instead of scooting to a cinema. Catching a film on the big screen is exciting but it can be as exciting when you watch it in the comfort of your own home.

52 - Go Backpacking

Retreat to somewhere peaceful regularly with items on your backpack. Doing so will remind you of the simple pleasures in life and allow you to be more appreciative of your time indoors.

53 - A Walk Is all It Takes

Walk to school or to the office. In favor of arriving in your destination through a car, letting your feet take you there is more fulfilling. It is cheaper, too.

54 - A Carwash of Your Own

Wash your own car. Hiring somebody else will spare you from the probably exhausting task but it is unnecessary and will just add to the roster of things you have to pay for.

55 - Prepare Your Own Meals

Do the meal preparation yourself. Letting another take the task may just herd in issues. For one, he may not be aware of your favorite flavors; for another, he may not incorporate a balanced meal.

56 - Water over Soda

Drink water. Although it may not be as satisfying and tasty as soda, it is the better choice. Apart from being healthier, it is also more affordable.

57 - Trim it, My Friend

Ask a friend to cut your hair for you. Rather than go to a parlor and let a professional work on your mane, select the free (and possibly more exciting) alternative.

58 - Your Laundry Is Yours

Wash your own clothes. Avoid paying for the task to be done for you. Especially if you have time to spare, it is practical to clean up after your own mess.

59 – Furniture No More

Get rid of extra furniture. If you have an extra couch or an extra bed, remind yourself that it is only eating space in your home. Consider giving it away or selling it on EBay.

60 – You Can Have It

Avoid starting a collection habit. . Memorabilia of movies or musicians, action figures, and exclusive luxuries? You are better off without any of them. As much of a fan as you are, take note that keeping these items is not ideal if you want to adopt a frugal life.

Chapter 7: Budgeting For Beginners

The essence of budgeting is often taken for granted, even though it is often the most common given to you if you intend to live with a set amount regularly. So, you won't be all over the place in the long run, monitoring how much you spend and what you spend on is the way to go. By maintaining control of your finances, you get to enjoy every cent you own.

61 - Coupons Are Your Friends

Search for coupons to online stores. Usually, plenty are available and grant special deals and discounts of up to 70%.

62 - Sticking to the Basics

Avoid purchase of fancy items. If you think about, you will do fine with just water, food, and clothes. Additionally, so long as you have a home to go to, you do not need anything else.

63 - Write, Write, Write

Take notes of your finances. Keep receipts, jot down the items you are set to purchase, and list your regular income, along with everything else regarding your expenses.

64 – News on the Net

Cancel newspaper and magazine subscriptions. Why? They cost a lot of money. Instead, gets updates on current events online. They are readily available and they are free.

65 – Do Not Cross the Line

Follow a budget. If you plan to spend $150 per week, be reminded not to take out more cash from your wallet when you have reached your quota. Be strict by telling yourself to stop purchasing items when you have gone overboard.

66 – A Movie on the Web

Download movies in favor of renting them. Take advantage of the digital inventions and save yourself the hassle of having to visit a movie rental store every time.

67 – The Melodies on the Internet

Listen to music online. Doing so can be done without having to pay a dime. Granted you have uninterrupted access to the internet, you can enjoy your favorite songs easily.

68 – Keep Your Towel on

Avoid washing towels too often. They will just be prone to damage if you have them laundered daily. Besides, they are usually clean, especially if you only use them after each bath time.

69 – Be Unique

Do not chase trends. For instance, if you are not even into baggy jeans, do not proceed with the purchase. Just because everybody else is wearing them does not mean you have to, too.

70 – No Ads, Please

Stay away from advertisements. Many of them are good in marketing. If you are not aware that something exists, you may not even want it.

Chapter 8: Decluttering Tips For Your Home

Your home is supposed to be your solace, not a place that curses you with a headache every time you look at it. Take the time to ensure that accessories, appliances, cabinets, desks and chairs, and furniture in each room are in order. Granted, you will not have to deal with the stress stitched with the mess. The bigger result? You will have more energy to focus on things that matter.

71 - Throw Them all Away

Do not be hesitant in throwing away stuff that cannot be of any use to you. They may still be in condition but since you do not need them, toss them onto the garbage. If you prefer, pass them onto a friend or a family member.

72 - Unleash Your Artsy Side

Be creative if you cannot seem to find value in what you have. Rather than go on a spree of purchasing a load of items, make use of what you already have.

73 - The Cleaner Way to Go

Clean your house. As simple as it is, you are less likely to feel the urge to go somewhere else if you have a pleasant and mess-free home.

74 – One Today, Another Tomorrow

Eliminate one item per day. If you have too many possessions you do not need, do not subject yourself to the stress of getting rid of them in one go. Do it gradually.

75 – Your Own Station

Have a desk. Especially if you are fond of scribbling notes, you may not help but scatter pieces of paper around the house. Unless, you have a table.

76 – A Remedy for Trash

Place trash baskets in every room. If you have cans that are easily accessible to be used for garbage, it is likely that your home will remain clean.

77 – Everything Needs a Home

Prepare a "home" for each item. You can get rid of clutter if you can return stuff back to their own space.

78 – Just Enough Cosmetics

Try not to purchase too many cosmetics (especially those in huge containers) such as make-up products and lotions - especially if you do not even use them often. They will only occupy an area supposed to be free.

79 – A Cabinet Here and a Cabinet There

Put cabinets inside each room. You may own a lot of belongings, which can be difficult to handle neatly. However, if you have drawers, you can tidy up sections of your home.

80 – Hello and Goodbye

Once you buy an item, get rid of something else. Rather than let them accumulate, pick something to let go.

81 – All-in-One

Choose multi-functional furniture. Countertops that can serve as a chair and a cabinet have been designed. They allow you to be savvy when it comes to the space inside your home.

Chapter 9: Organization Techniques For Your Home

Aside from the fact that it enhances the looks, a reason to organize your home is for practicality's sake - for you to save time and even money. Remember, with a well-kept home, you would know exactly where your stuff is and you won't have to purchase a new set.

Take for example the time you cannot find your screwdriver. Did it take you more than an hour to search just about every drawer in the house for it? Then, since it's nowhere to be found, you consume another hour scooting to the hardware to buy a new one. Those hours could have been used to take a nap, watch your favorite TV shows, prepare yourself a ham sandwich, or whatever you want. Instead, they went to waste.

82 – Compartmentalization

Categorize your belongings. Use boxes of various sizes especially if you keep little things that can be challenging to find in the future.

83 – A Color of Its Own

If applicable, sort things according to their color. This can also work when choosing a theme for rooms. For example, you can opt for a rustic-style kitchen, or use pastels for your living room.

84 – As You Go

Always clean after creating a mess. Avoid putting off the chore for later because, chances are, you will not be returning to them.

85 – A Pile of Clothes

As soon as you take off your clothes, hang or put them in a hamper. Do not just leave them on the bed or scattered on the floor.

86 – In Your Own Time

Establish a home-organization routine. Do you prefer to arrange all items once a week? Or, do you want to clean a portion (i.e. kitchen, bathroom, living room) in a day, then, move on to another portion the next day? Everything is all up to you and your schedule.

87 – Spice Things Up

Re-arrange furniture regularly. Treat your home to a makeover every now and then since it will make you feel excited to hang out inside, although it is where you lurk most of the time.

88 – A Jar for Everything

Be ready with little jars. For example, set aside a jar for old coins. This way you will know exactly where to look when you are hunting for the specific item.

89 – A Few Will Do

Limit how many home décors you put up. The idea is to live simply, right? Try to tone it down with the designs inside your home.

#90 – NO to Dirty Dishes

Wash dishes daily. Avoid letting dirty dishes add up. For one, doing so is unsanitary. For another, cleaning the mess left on them for days will consume more time – time you should much rather be spending on other things.

91 – Don't Forget the Fridge

Arrange your fridge. Instead of just allowing food and other edibles to be caught in a jumble, set everything in order. This way, you will have a clear view of every item you have.

Chapter 10: Maintaining Frugal Simplicity

Knowing how to be frugal is as essential as knowing that you are capable of continuing your progress as you adopt a frugal lifestyle. Truth be told, maintaining your new practice is the tricky part. However, if you are willing to have what it takes, the struggle cannot put your flame out. If you really want to live a frugal life, nothing can stop you.

92 - Ride a Bike

Regularly, take time to ride a bike. Doing so is enjoyable and frees your mind from stress. Additionally, it is a good means of exercise.

93 - Especially for You

Give out hand-made presents. Instead of getting a gift that can be bought easily from a store, take a moment to make others an item only you can make. For one, they are cheaper; for another, your loved ones will appreciate them better.

94 - No Room for More Pets

Avoid adopting pets. They may be adorable and having them around can be worthwhile. However, raising them can be costly.

95 – On Buying Items: Patience Is a Virtue

Learn to wait for the best moment to buy items. Usually, stores set schedules for grand sales. Since you can avail of great promos on those days, put off your purchases.

96 - A Break at the Right Place and at the Right Time

Take vacations during the right months. Airlines and hotels have cheap deals regularly.

97 - A Smoker No More

Stop smoking. Not only is it detrimental to your health, as well as to the health of those around you, it can be an expensive habit.

98 - Adopt the DIY Ethic

Instead of turning to a professional, fix stuff yourself. Let's say, the fan in your room stopped working. Figure out a way to have it repaired. If it gets broken again eventually, you can attend to it the second time around.

99 – NO to Whines

Avoid complaining. Try not to consume energy focusing on negative aspects. If you think something is unfair, do something about it. Otherwise, learn to settle.

100 – Yours to Appreciate

Enjoy items even if you are not their owner. Take for example, fine art displayed in museums. Be okay with the fact that you can still take pleasure in simply laying eyes on them.

101 – You Are on Top

Have your own meaning of success. If being successful means being happy doing minor tasks, try not to be bummed out if it is not how another perceives it.

Conclusion

Thank you again for purchasing the book *Frugal Simplicity: 101 Ways To Use Frugal Simplicity For Organizing And Decluttering Your Life And Embracing The Simplicity Lifestyle For Greater Personal Finances And Freedom.*

Hopefully, this e-book has helped you discover that it is not difficult to adopt and maintain a frugal lifestyle. So long as you are willing to correct some practices and you are determined to continue your progress, you can make it happen.

Now that you know the secrets, as well as the many exciting possibilities that come along, on frugality, you can begin the journey to a frugal path. To paraphrase what Benjamin Franklin said, you will see the best in everything and are likely to be more content if you value the essence of frugality: of doing whatever you can, with what you have and where you are.

Please don't be someone who just reads this information and doesn't apply it, the strategies in this book will only benefit you if you use them!

If you know of anyone else that could benefit from the information presented here please inform them of this book.

Finally, if you enjoyed this book and feel it has added value to your life in any way, please take the time to share your thoughts and post a review on Amazon. It'd be greatly appreciated!

Thank you and good luck!

Preview Of:

<u>Minimalism</u>

Discover Minimalism, Declutter, And Be Stress Free Living The Lifestyle Of Simplicity In 10 Easy Steps!

Introduction

I want to thank you and congratulate you for purchasing the book, "Minimalism: Discover Minimalism, Declutter, And Be Stress Free Living The Lifestyle Of Simplicity In 10 Easy Steps!". This "Minimalism" book contains proven steps and strategies on how to apply the principle of minimalism in your life so that you can have a happy and meaningful life that is devoid of distractions and stress.

Minimalism entails a person to live only with the barest necessities so that he may ultimately focus on those things that he truly enjoys. For someone who is utterly consumed by material things and is drowned by a hectic lifestyle, embracing minimalism is definitely a daunting task. As such, this book is here to help you transform each day of your life from chaos into peace.

The book consists of ten chapters, which basically will answer these three fundamental questions about minimalism:

- What is minimalism?
- How can you be a minimalist?
- Can you sustain a minimalist lifestyle?

Upon unraveling the answers to these three key questions, hopefully this book can help you transform your life into a clutter-free and stress-free one by just following ten easy steps towards a minimalistic life.

Thanks again for purchasing this book, I hope you enjoy it!

Chapter 1: Reasons Behind Living A Minimalist Lifestyle

Consumerism has become entwined in everyone's lives. As you open your television for the first time during the day, after every segment of your favorite morning show you are exposed to ads about products that claim you need them, when in fact you have lived your whole life just fine without them. As you get into your car and head for work, you are still bombarded by ads – on the sidewalks, in billboards, and in posters. Advertisements are everywhere.

Ads Convert your Wants to Needs

As a consumer, for every single thing that you have, you want it to be the best. You want to achieve perfection in every way, such as having fashionable outfit, getting the trendy shoes and bags, or buying the latest gadgets. That's why advertisements lure you into buying their products through these fantasies of yours. As an example, look at these taglines and see if you aren't caught up with these brands until now.

KFC: It's finger lickin' good!

Mac Pro: Beauty outside. Beast inside.

Survivor: Outwit. Outplay. Outlast.

Disneyland: The happiest place on earth.

M&M's: Melts in your mouth, not in your hands.

Along with their catchy taglines, these brands are big spenders in marketing justto promote their products. Apple, for instance, enhances the aesthetics of their stores to entice people to come in and try their stuff. Even without a commercial, M&M's play into your imaginations through their tagline "melts in your mouth, not in your hands". All of these advertisements are created so that you will think that the product or service that a company is selling is a "need" rather than a "want".

You're Stressed on the Excesses in Your Life

Now, try to search inside of your home for any items that you may not have used for the past month. The mere idea of having items you do not use frequently is a sign that you may be accumulating things that are way past your necessity.

That's the main reason why people these days are more stressed than ever. They take in excessive things in their life. The more stuff you have, the lesser space there is in your house and more things you have to clean. In your daily lives in your home, school, or work, more work for you each day meant less time for breaks and more stress on your part.

These are the very reasons on why minimalism should become relevant for everyone. Minimalism removes these excesses in life so that one can live simply and happy.

Thanks for Previewing My Exciting Book Entitled:

"Minimalism: Discover Minimalism, Declutter, And Be Stress Free Living The Lifestyle Of Simplicity In 10 Easy Steps!"

To purchase this book, simply go to the Amazon Kindle store and simply search:

"MINIMALISM"

Then just scroll down until you see my book. You will know it is mine because you will see my name "Lilly Sparks" underneath the title.

Alternatively, you can visit my author page on Amazon to see this book and other work I have done. Thanks so much, and please don't forget your free bonuses

DON'T LEAVE YET! - CHECK OUT YOUR FREE BONUSES BELOW!

Free Bonus Offer: Get Free Access To The www.LuxyLifeNaturals.comVIP Newsletter!

Once you enter your email address you will immediately get free access to this awesome newsletter!

But wait, right now if you join now for free you will also get free access to the "Anti-Aging Made Easy" free EBook!

To claim both your FREE VIP NEWSLETTER MEMBERSHIP and your FREE BONUS Ebook on ANTI-AGING MADE EASY!

Just Go To:

www.LuxyLifeNaturals.com

www.ingramcontent.com/pod-product-compliance
Lightning Source LLC
Chambersburg PA
CBHW070754180526
45168CB00004B/1606